HEART A
New Songs from
Ally McBeal

5. **Read Your Mind**

9. **100 Tears Away**

13. **Someday We'll Be Together**

17. **To Sir, With Love**
(Duet With Al Green)

20. **Sweet Inspiration**

24. **Crying**

29. **Vincent (Starry Starry Night)**

32. **What Becomes Of The Brokenhearted**

37. **Confetti**

40. **Baby, Don't You Break My Heart Slow**
(Duet with Emily Saliers of the Indigo Girls)

46. **This Is Crazy Now**

51. **This Old Heart Of Mine**
(Is Weak For You)

54. **I Know Him By Heart**

Bonus Track
57. **Searchin' My Soul**

International
MUSIC
Publications

INTERNATIONAL MUSIC PUBLICATIONS LIMITED

ENGLAND: GRIFFIN HOUSE,
161 HAMMERSMITH ROAD, LONDON W6 8BS
GERMANY: MARSTALLSTR. 8. D-80539 MUNCHEN
DENMARK: DANMUSIK, VOGNMAGERGADE 7
DK 1120 KOBENHAVN

WARNER/CHAPPELL MUSIC

CANADA: 85 SCARSDALE ROAD, SUITE 101
DON MILLS, ONTARIO, M3B 2R2

SCANDINAVIA: P.O. BOX 533, VENDEVAGEN 85 B
S-182 15, DANDERYD, SWEDEN

AUSTRALIA: P.O. BOX 353
3 TALAVERA ROAD, NORTH RYDE N.S.W. 2113

Nuova CARISH S.p.A.

ITALY: NUOVA CARISCH SRL, VIA CAMPANIA 12
20098 SAN GIULIANO MILANESE, MILANO

FRANCE: CARISCH MUSICOM
25 RUE D'HAUTEVILLE, 75010 PARIS

SPAIN: NUEVA CARISCH ESPAÑA
MAGALLANES 25, 28015 MADRID
www.carisch.com

WARNER BROS. PUBLICATIONS
THE GLOBAL LEADER IN PRINT

USA: 15800 NW 48TH AVENUE, MIAMI, FL 33014

Music Transcribed by Artemis Music Limited, Pinewood Road, Iver Heath, Bucks SL0 0NH
Printed by The Panda Group · Haverhill · Suffolk CB9 8PR · UK · Binding by Haverhill Print Finishers

Read Your Mind

We held hands and laughed
Then we jumped in the water
Off the jetty we'd fly
As the sun got hotter
We were any age
Floating through space
Happy for once in the human race
On this sweet Sunday, and into Monday
Your arms wrapped around me
Where my love has found me
Has finally found me
But am I really free?

If I could read your mind
I hope I'd find
The same love I have in mine
If I could go back in time
I'd try to find you
And make up for all this wasted time

Like a broken record
I've stayed protected
From promises, from disappointments
I wanna hear your dreams, wanna drift away
Wanna break you in
Oh I wanna stay
Stay in heaven, oh in heaven
And see my life finally begin
Will we be together, oh forever?
Darling please let me in

If I could read your mind
I hope I'd find
The same love I have in mine
If I could go back in time
I'd try to find you
And make up for all this wasted time

Oh I want to stay in this sweet Sunday, and into Monday
Your arms wrapped around me
Where my love has found me
Has finally found me
But am I really free?

If I could read your mind
I hope I'd find
The same love I have in mine
If I could go back in time
I'd try to find you
And make up for all this wasted time
Na, na, na, na, na...

If I could read your mind
(Na, na, na, na, na...)

This Old Heart Of Mine (Is Weak For You)

Oh, this old heart of mine
Been broke a thousand times
Each time you break away
I feel you're gonna stay
Lonely nights that come
Memories that flow
Bringing you back again
Hurting me more and more
Maybe it's my mistake to show this love I feel inside
Cause each day that passes by
You got me never knowing if I'm coming or going, but I

I love you
This old heart darling (darling) weeps for you
I love you, yes I do (yes I do)

These old arms of mine
Miss having you around
Makes these tears inside
Start falling down, well
Always with half a kiss
You remind me of what I miss
So I try to control myself
Like I'm gonna start fainting cause my heart stops beating, cause I

I love you
This old heart darling weeps for you (weeps for you)
I love you, yes I do (yes I do)

Oh I try to hide my hurt inside
This old heart of mine always makes me cry
The way you treat me leaves me incomplete
You're in for the day, gone for the week, now
But if you leave me a hundred times
A hundred times I'll take you back
I'm yours whenever you want me
I'm not too proud to shout it
To tell the world about it, cause I

I love you
This old heart darling (darling) weeps for you
I love you
This old heart darling weeps for you (weeps for you)
I love you
This old heart darling (darling) weeps for you
I love you, yes I do (yes I do)

Sweet Inspiration

I need your sweet inspiration
I need you here on my mind
Every hour of the day
Without your sweet inspiration
The lonely hours of the night
Just don't go my way

A woman in love
Needs sweet inspiration
Yeah, and honey that's all I ask, that's all I ask from you
I've gotta have your sweet inspiration
You know there just ain't no tellin' what a satisfied woman might do

The way you call me baby, baby
Is such a sweet inspiration
The way you call me darlin', darlin'
Sets my heart to skating
And if I'm out in the rain, baby
And in a bad situation
You know I just reach back in my mind
And there I find your sweet, sweet inspiration

Sweet inspiration
Oh, what a power
And I've got the power
Every hour of the day
I need your sweet inspiration
To go on, to go on living
To keep on giving this way

I need your sweet inspiration
Sweet inspiration, sweet inspiration, sweet inspiration
Sweet, sweet inspiration
Sweet, sweet inspiration
I need, sweet inspiration

Baby, Don't You Break My Heart Slow (Duet with Emily Saliers of the Indigo Girls)

I like the way you wanted me
Every night for so long baby
I like the way you needed me
Every time things got rocky

I was believing in you
Was I mistaken
Do you say, do you say what you mean?
I want our love to last forever

But I'd rather you be mean than love and lie
I'd rather hear the truth and have to say goodbye
I'd rather take a blow at least then I would know
But baby don't you break my heart slow

I like the way you'd hold me
Every night for so long baby
And like the way you'd say my name
In the middle of the night
While you were sleeping

I was believing in you
Was I mistaken
Do you mean, do you mean what you say?
When you say our love could last forever

But I'd rather you be mean than love and lie
I'd rather hear the truth and have to say goodbye
I'd rather take a blow at least then I would know
But baby don't you break my heart slow

You would run around and lead me on forever
While I wait at home still thinking that we're together
I wanted our love to last forever
I was believing in you

I'd rather you be mean then love and lie
I'd rather hear the truth and have to say goodbye
I'd rather take a blow at least then I would know
But baby don't you break my heart slow

This Is Crazy Now

Blown like the wind, restless again
My only friend has gone away
Washed like the tide but I'm still alive
I'm gonna drive all night long

This is crazy now, I'll fill the space somehow
If there were someway to get through
This is crazy now, I'll fill the space somehow
I can't walk away from you

Shaken like a leaf, sharpened like a reef
All of my senses need relief
Looking out to sea, I still believe
That you and I were meant to be

This is crazy now, I'll fill the space somehow
If there were someway to get through
This is crazy now (like finger paint)
I'll fill the space somehow (smearing in the rain)
I can't walk away from you (wash it all away)

This is crazy now (shaken like a leaf)
I'll fill the space somehow (sharpened like a reef)
I can't walk away from you

This is crazy now
(Shaken like a leaf)
I'll fill the space somehow
(Sharpened like a reef)
I can't walk away from you

Vincent (Starry Starry Night)

Starry, starry night
Paint your palette blue and gray
Look out on a summer's day
With eyes that know the darkness in my soul
Shadows on the hill
Sketch the trees and daffodils
Catch the breeze and the winter chills
In colors on the snowy linen land

Now I understand
What you tried to say to me
And how you suffered your sanity
And how you tried to set them free
They would not listen, they did not know how
Perhaps they'll listen now

Starry, starry night
Flaming flowers that brightly blaze
Swirling clouds in violet haze
Reflect in Vincent's eyes of China blue
Colors changing hue
Morning fields of amber grain
Weathered faces lined in pain
Are soothed beneath the artist's loving hand

Now I understand
What you tried to say to me
They did not listen, they did not know how
Perhaps they'll listen now
Starry, starry night

Crying

I was alright for awhile
I could smile for awhile
But I saw you last night
You held my hand so tight
As you stopped to say "hello" Oh you wished me
You couldn't tell that I'd been

Crying for you
Crying over you
When you said, "so long"
Left me standing all alone
Alone and crying
Crying, crying, crying, crying
It's hard to understand
How the touch of your hand
Can start me crying

I thought that I was over you
But it's true, oh so true
I love you even more
Than I did before
But darling what can I do?
For you don't love me
And I'll always be
Crying for you
Crying for you

Yes now you're gone
And from this moment on
I'll be crying, crying, crying, crying
Yes crying
Crying
Over you

O Tears Away

...head and cry now
...give into the madness
...only way to feel your joy
...st to feel your sadness

...head and sail now
...give into the ocean
...only way to tame your fear
...feel her rocky motion

...re a long way from somewhere you call home, yeah
...e's a place in your heart, you're not alone
...f the happiness you seek
...f the joy for which you pray
...ser than you think
...ist 100 tears away

...head and listen
...give into the voices
...think you're backed into the corner
...ou've got so many choices
...re a long way from someplace you feel safe
...e of mind comes from just one place
...f the happiness you seek
...f the joy for which you pray
...ser than you think
...st 100 tears away

...re a long way from somewhere you call home,
...e's a place in your heart, you're not alone
...f the happiness you seek
...f the joy for which you pray
...ser than you think
...ist 100 tears away
...ever it is that'll make you feel good
...an have if you want
...u knew that you could
...loser than you think
...ist 100 tears away

...neday We'll Be Together

...day we'll be together
...say it, say it, say it, say it again)
...day we'll be together
...yes we will, yes we will)

...e far away, baby
...me my love, ooh yeah
...ust as sure my, my baby
...ere are stars above
...na say

...day we'll be together
...yes we will, yes we will)
...day, some sweet day
...be together
...I know, I know, I know, I know)

...ve is yours, baby
...from the start, oh yeah
...you, you possess my soul now honey
...w, I know you own my heart
...wanna say

...day, some sweet day
...be together
...es we will, yes we will)
...day, tell everybody
...be together
...I know)
...g time ago, my, my sweet thing
...de a big mistake honey
...I I, said goodbye
...bye, bye, bye)
...r, ever, ever)
..., and ever, and ever)
...since that day now
...all I wanna do
...wanna do
..., cry, cry

...for you
..., every night
...just to kiss your sweet lips baby
...you ever, and ever so tight, and I wanna say

...day, some sweet day
...be together
...yes we will, yes we will)
...day we'll be together
...know, I know, I know, I know, I know)
...day we'll be together
...e will, yes we will)
...day we'll be together

Confetti

Skinny little brats
Walking down Avenue A
Dangling their cigarettes
Their Independence Day
Tears like filigrees
Wear them on their sleeves
Nobody's main squeeze
It's thirty-five degrees

Poetry of ordinary life is what I live for
They just wanna be seen
They just wanna be heard...said

My words are like confetti
And you never pick them up
They fall to the ground
I need someone to lift me up

So diaphanous so ephemeral
And all those bad words
They never learned in school
Groovy like my mama was
In her black turtleneck
She was so high-strung
She was so low tech

Poetry and tattooed dreams
And fourteen carat nose rings
The children of elite
Are trying to be street saying

My words are like confetti
And you never pick them up
They fall to the ground
I need someone to lift me up

Repeat chorus

To Sir, With Love
(Duet with Al Green)

The time has come
For closing books, and long last looks must end
And as I leave
I know that I am leaving my best friend
A friend who taught me right from wrong
And weak from strong
That's a lot to learn
What, what can I give you in return?

If you wanted the moon
I would try to make a start
But I, would rather let me give my heart
To you, with love

Those schoolgirl days
Of telling tales and biting nails are gone, yeah
But in my mind
I know that they live on and on and on and on
But how do you thank someone
Who has taken you from crayons to perfume?
Well it's not easy
But I'll try

If you wanted the sky
I would write across the sky in letters
That would soar a thousand feet high
To you, with love
Those awkward years have hurried by
Why did they fly, fly away?
Why is it Sir children, grow up to be people one day?
What takes the place of climbing trees and dirty knees in the world outside?
What, what is there that I can buy?

If you wanted the world
I'd surround it with a wall I'd scrawl
These words with letters ten feet tall
To you, with love

What Becomes Of The Brokenhearted

As I walk this land of broken dreams
I have visions of many things
Love's happiness is just an illusion
Filled with sadness and confusion

What becomes of the brokenhearted
Who had love that's now departed
I know I've got to find
Some kind of peace of mind, maybe
The fruits of love grow all around
But for me they come tumbling down
Everyday heartaches grow a little stronger
I can't stand this pain much longer
I walk in shadows searching for light
Cold and alone, no comfort in sight
Hoping and praying for someone to care
Always moving and going nowhere

What becomes of the brokenhearted
Who had love that's now departed
I know I've got to find
Some kind of peace of mind, baby

I'm searching though I don't succeed
But someone look, there's a growing need
Oh he is lost, there's no place for beginning
All that's left is an unhappy ending

Now what becomes of the brokenhearted
Who had love that's now departed
I know I've got to find
Some kind of peace of mind
I'll be searching everywhere
Just to find someone to care
I'll be looking every day
I know I'm gonna find a way
Nothing's gonna stop me now
I will find a way somehow

I Know Him By Heart

There's a secret path I follow
To a place no one can find
Where I meet my perfect someone
I've kept hidden in my mind
Where my heart makes my decisions
'Till my dream becomes a vision
And the love I feel
Makes him real someday

Cause I know he's out there somewhere
Just beyond my reach
Though I've never really touched him
Or ever heard him speak
Though we've never been together
We've never been apart
No we've never met
Haven't found him yet
But I know him by heart

Am I living an illusion?
Wanting something I can't see
If I compromise, I'd be living lies
Pretending love's not meant to be
Cause I know my heart's worth saving
And I know that he'll be waiting
So I'll hold on and I'll stay strong 'till then

Cause I know he's out there somewhere
Just beyond my reach
Though I've never really touched him
Or ever heard him speak
Though we've never been together
We've never been apart

No we've never met
Haven't found him yet
But I know him by heart
No we've never met
Haven't found him yet
But I know it by heart

Read Your Mind

Words by Vonda Shepard
Music by Mitchell Froom and Vonda Shepard

1. We held hands and laughed then we jumped in the wa - ter; off the jet - ty we'd fly
2. Like a bro - ken re - cord I've stayed pro - tect - ed from pro - mi - ses

as the sun got hot - ter. We were a - ny age, float - ing through space, hap - py for once
from dis - ap - point - ments. I wan - na hear your dreams, wan - na drift a - way, wan - na break you in.

6

100 Tears Away

Words and Music by
Vonda Shepard and Paul Gordon

1. Go a - head and cry now, just give in to the mad - ness.
2. Go a - head and sail now, just give in to the o - cean.
(Verse 3 see block lyric)

The on - ly way to feel your joy is first to feel sad-
The on - ly way to tame your fear is to feel her rock - ing
4° instrumental

it's just a hun - - dred tears a - way. ___

Verse 3:
Go ahead and listen
Just give in to the voices.
You think you're backed into the corner
But you've got so many choices.
You're a long way from some place you feel safe.
Peace of mind comes from just one place.
All of the happiness you seek
All of the joy for which you pray
Is closer than you think:
It's just a hundred tears away.

Someday We'll Be Together

Words and Music by
Jackey Beavers, John Bristol and Harvey Fuqua

Some - day____ we'll be to - geth ___ ___ ___ er.

Some - day____ we'll be to - geth ___ ___ ___ er.

To Sir, With Love

Words by Don Black
Music by Marc London

Verse 2:

Those awkward years have hurried by;

Why did they fly, fly away?

Why is it, Sir, children grow up to be people one day?

What takes the place of climbing trees and dirty knees in the world outside?

What, what is there I can buy?

If you wanted the world

I'd surround it with a wall. I'd scrawl

These words with letters ten feet tall:

"To you, with love."

Sweet Inspiration

Words and Music by
Dan Penn and Spooner Oldham

Crying

Words and Music by
Roy Orbison and Joe Melson

I was al - right for a while,_____ I could smile for a while; but I saw you last night,— you held my hand so tight as you stopped to say__ hel - lo._____ Oh you wished me__ well,__ you

Vincent (Starry Starry Night)

Words and Music by
Don McLean

Verse 3:
Starry, starry night
Flaming flowers that brightly blaze
Swirling clouds in violet haze
Reflect in Vincent's eyes of China Blue.

Verse 4:
Colours changing hue
Morning fields of amber grain
Weathered faces lined in pain
Are smoothed beneath the artist's loving hand.

What Becomes Of The Brokenhearted

Words and Music by
James Dean, Paul Riser and
William Weatherspoon

Confetti

Words and Music by
Vonda Shepard

1. Skin-ny lit-tle brats walk-ing down A-ven-ue A, dan-gl-ing their ci-gar-ettes,
2. So di-a-pha-nous, so e - phe-me-ral and all those bad words
3. *Instrumental*

their In-de-pen-dence Day. Tears like fi-li-grees, wear them on their sleeves,
they nev-er learned at school; groo-vy like me ma-ma was, in a black tur-tle-neck,

Baby, Don't You Break My Heart Slow

Words by Vonda Shepard
Music by Vonda Shepard and
James Newton Howard

I wait at home still think-ing we're to-geth-er. I want-ed our love to last for-

-ev - er.

(ad lib. vocal)

This Is Crazy Now

Words and Music by
Vonda Shepard

This Old Heart Of Mine
(Is Weak For You)

Words and Music by
Sylvia Moy, Brian Holland,
Eddie Holland and Lamont Dozier

I Know Him By Heart

Words and Music by
Paul Williams and Jon Vezner

1. There's a se - cret path I fol - low to a place no - one can find,
2. Am I liv - ing an il - lu - sion, want - ing some - thing I can't see? If I

where I meet my per - fect some - one I've kept hid - den
com - pro - mise, I'd be liv - ing lies, pre - tend - ing love's not

in my mind, where my heart makes my de - ci - sions till my
meant to be. 'Cause I know my heart's worth sav - ing, and I

Searchin' My Soul

Words and Music by
Vonda Shepard

1. I've been down this road, walk-in' the line
2. One by one, the chains a-round

that's paint-ed by pride.
me un-wind.

And I have made mis-takes
Ev-ery-day now,

Printed in England
The Panda Group · Haverhill · Suffolk · 4/00

ALSO AVAILABLE

Available from all good music stores.

For a free catalogue containing details of IMP's extensive range of music products, please write to the address below stating your areas of interest:

International Music Publications Limited
Griffin House, 161 Hammersmith Road, London W6 8BS, England